Free-Style Quilts

A "No Rules" Approach

Susan Carlson

C&T PUBLISHING

Copyright © 2000 Susan E. Carlson
Illustrations © 2000 C&T Publishing
Development Editor: Cyndy Lyle Rymer
Technical Editor: Lynn Koolish
Copy Editor: Vera Tobin
Book Design: Ewa Gavrielov
Cover Design/Production: Kris Yenche
Graphic Illustrations: Norman Remer
Cover Images: Details of the author's quilts *Emerald Swallowtail* (page 70), *Ocean Tide Grouper* (page 27), and *Echinacea and Black-eyed Susans* (page 15).
Back cover images: *Calla Lillies*, Judy Marble (page 13), and *Dos Picados*, Holly Ranone (page 80). The copyrights on individual artworks are retained by the artist.
Unless otherwise noted, all photographs by Andrew Edgar Photography, Portsmouth, New Hampshire.

We take great care to ensure that the information included in this book is accurate and presented in good faith, but no warranty is provided nor results guaranteed. Since we have no control over the choice of materials or procedures used, neither the author nor C&T Publishing, Inc. shall have any liability to any person or entity with respect to any loss or damage caused directly or indirectly by the information contained in this book.

Attention Teachers: C&T Publishing, Inc. encourages you to use this book as a text for teaching. Contact us at 800-284-1114 or www.ctpub.com for more information about the C&T Teachers Program.

Trademarked (™) and Registered Trademarked (®) names are used throughout this book. Rather than use the symbols with every occurrence of a trademark and registered trademark name, we have only used the symbol the first time the product appears. We are using the names only in an editorial fashion and to the benefit of the owner, with no intention of infringement.

Library of Congress Cataloging-in-Publication Data

Carlson, Susan E.
  Free-style quilts : a "no rules" approach / Susan E. Carlson.
    p. cm.
Includes index.
  ISBN 1-57120-102-5 (paper trade)
1. Quilting--Patterns. 2. Appliqué--Patterns. I. Title.
  TT835 .C37412 2000
  746.46'041--dc21
                                    99-050975

Published by C&T Publishing, Inc.
P.O. Box 1456
Lafayette, California 94549

Printed in China
10 9 8 7 6 5 4 3

Contents

Dedication

To Mama and Daddy

Snooks
Susan Carlson, 21½" × 30", 1991.
Collection of William and Meta Carlson.
Portrait of the artist—as a young girl.

Acknowledgments

First, I need to thank my loving and patient husband, Tom Allen, without whose support and expertise this book would never have reached the proposal stage, much less become a finished manuscript. This is as much your book as it is mine. Thank you so much.

To my family, an eternal thank you for your ever-present love and encouragement, and for providing me with wonderful examples of creativity and ingenuity. We may not live near each other, but you are always in my heart.

Thanks to Andrew Edgar for his photography through the years and *especially* during the last few months of preparation for this book.

To the Renegades present and past. You have all added timely inspiration, advice, and instruction. Meeting with you has influenced me and my art in ways I can never measure. Thank you for pursuing your own muses and inspiring mine.

Thanks to all the students who submitted work—I wish I could have included all of them—and to the students and customers who requested this book in the first place, and who give me impetus to keep the fabric flying.

To Portsmouth Fabric Company for providing friendly faces, a home-away-from-home, and a fabric selection that has fueled many a quilt.

To our friends who have encouraged, supported, and inspired both me and Tom in our art. Thanks for the hours upon hours of critique and camaraderie we have shared through the years.

And thank you, Sam, for teaching me what unconditional love—and time-management—is all about.

Mackerel
Susan Carlson, 14 ¾" x 12", 1994–?.
For Tom—a work in perpetual progress.

S Carlson ©1996

chapter one

Fabric Collage: Learning to Let Go

Fabric collage is a technique that developed almost spontaneously out of my love for fabric. I love all kinds of fabrics: cotton and rayon, batik and upholstery. My first experiences with fabric were purely experimental. I made clothes and quilts for my dolls, and later strip-pieced scraps into blocks for larger quilts. I had no idea that you were supposed to use all the same type of fabric in such creations, so those early quilts contain cottons of all makes and weights, polyesters and double-knits, heavy upholstery prints and silky lining fabrics. If it was in the scrap basket it was fair game. And pre-washing? What's that?

The essence of fabric collage is this: Cut fabric the size and shape you want and tack it in place with glue. Keep adding fabric, layer upon layer, until you have created the image you desire. Then construct the quilt much like any other—sandwich cotton batting between the top and a backing, quilt through the layers with different colored threads, and finish the edges.

It's that simple, yet I understand how difficult it can be mentally—to let go of the rules of quilting. To learn that there are no limits. I feel lucky to have approached quilting without having taken a beginning quilting class. When I did learn the "rules," I felt secure enough to follow the ones that worked for me, and to bend or even break others.

"Don't leave any rough edges."

"Don't use glue on fabric."

These are the two big rules that are the most difficult to ignore. But these are at the heart of fabric collage. Cutting fabric pieces to exact sizes and gluing them down—rather than figuring in seam allowances and painstakingly sewing abutting pieces together—is a liberating and exciting process. It is liberating because of the ease with which you can try options and make changes. And it is exciting because, at some level, a wall is broken down.

The permission to play and the encouragement to explore—ways of breaking down the wall—are the most important things I can give my students. I tell them to rely instead on their own ideas and intuition. Students tell me again and again that my class frees them to do and try things they thought they couldn't do with fabric.

Gobi Gecko
Susan Carlson, 13 ½" x 18", 1996.
Collection of Rosemarie Grimes. An off-shoot of fish: lizards, salamanders, and in this case, a gecko. Another example of the great shapes and colors found in nature.

I can't deny that an art background helps in creating images with fabric. I took many classes even before attending art college. This education gave me a strong foundation in drawing and interpreting visual images onto two-dimensional surfaces. However, someone without an arts education can create images that are equally imaginative, creative, and artistic. Anyone with a desire to create should do so, regardless of their training.

All art is good art—if the heart of the artist is in it.

In fact, most of my students have not had any training in art. Yet, as you will see throughout this book, their work is creative and fun. Many have boldly set off into uncharted water to create works that I could not have imagined when I taught them this technique. In effect, they have made this technique their own. Many, in fact, have combined fabric collage with other techniques, including beading, reverse appliqué, silk ribbon embroidery, and clothing.

A Quilter's Journey

I'm often asked, "Where did you ever get the idea to do this?" Unfortunately, I don't have a concise answer. Inspiration and creativity come from many sources —from life experiences, family, friends, classes, pictures, articles, music, and so on. The technique of fabric collage didn't come to me in a dream. There was no one moment when the lights went on and I said "Ah hah!" Instead, the way I work has developed over many years and its story is the story of my development as an artist.

My first influences were my parents, of course, and the creativity they displayed in their crafts. My father is a woodworker. My mother is a seamstress and a quilter. They encouraged me to explore any avenue of expression that interested me. I spent years dabbling in just about every art and craft medium available—collage, decoupage, macramé, pottery, paper maché, batik, and so on.

My mother is an accomplished seamstress, and surely could have given me a myriad of rules to follow, but I can't remember any. We discovered quilting around the same time in the 70s. I followed her lead with strip-quilting, but soon started "skewing" the angles, so most blocks looked more like crazy quilts than stripped blocks. And patterns? Those were what you used for clothing, not quilting. I credit this early permission to experiment—with any sort of creative expression—with the development of the technique that you will be learning about.

I started using fabric as an artistic medium in college. I created a landscape using a traditional machine appliqué process, with a little beading thrown in. I also worked on a series of multimedia portraits of my parents and grandparents, using watercolors, inks, pastel pencils, embroidery floss, fabric, lace, and buttons.

Colorado Landscape
Susan Carlson, 26" × 37", 1983. Collection of the artist.

Tom
Susan Carlson, 18½" × 18", 1986. Collection of the artist.

Later, after a summer trip, I made a shadow-quilted piece based on a photo of a friend. I was satisfied with the result. But making a pattern based on a sketch and painstakingly cutting pieces didn't have the immediacy necessary to truly keep me interested. However, I stored away for the future the shadow-quilting technique of stitching through a top layer of tulle to hide the raw edges of appliqué underneath.

Then I tried freehand machine quilting. I lightly drew images in pencil onto muslin, layered the top with batting and backing, lowered the feed dogs on the machine, and away I went. What fun it was—like sketching with thread onto the fabric.

After taking an appliqué class that encouraged freehand cutting of fabric, I made a shadow-quilted portrait of my father-in-law, Dain, using freehand cutting and freehand machine quilting. I used remnants from my mother's closets and discarded fabrics from friends.

Dain
Susan Carlson, 33½" × 28", 1990.
Collection of Dain Allen.

At first, I played it safe with fabric selection, particularly in faces, using solids or translucent fabrics with very little pattern in them. Perhaps it was that one piece of plaid in Dain's face that inspired me, but as I produced more work and collected more fabric, I used more interesting and challenging prints. I went on to experiment with the patterns in fabrics, trying to use them to give volume and contour to faces. I was getting closer to the result I wanted, but still didn't think I was there.

With *Elements* I completed the development of fabric collage. A local quilt guild challenge to depict the four elements—earth, air, fire, and water—inspired me to try a personification of each. This proved a challenge for me on several levels. Since this piece was a composite of many photos of all different sizes and formats, keeping a cohesive look would be difficult. To solve my problem I used my husband's computer and Adobe Photoshop® software. He scanned in the images and showed me how to manipulate them, then I spent a weekend glued to the computer. I resized the photos so they would be similar in scale. Then I combined, flipped, and rotated them to create the design I wanted. I removed sunglasses from one subject. I even changed the coloring from "natural" to shades of red, blue, yellow, and green. The color printout I worked from is shown here.

Once the design was set, I came to the really fun part: fabric selection. As is evident, I changed flesh-tones to reflect a rainbow of colors. To my initial disappointment, my fabric collection was much more subdued than what I had in mind. But then I realized it was a great excuse for a fabric splurge! I shopped for the brightest, clearest patterns and colors I could find. My fabric collection has never been the same since.

From there, the piecing process was the same as I have described before—freehand cutting and tacking the pieces in place with glue. After searching out such wonderful and bright fabrics, however, I didn't want to subdue them by covering the piece with tulle for shadow quilting. I started machine quilting, raw edges and all. I had to do more quilting to make sure I hit every edge of every piece to hold them in place, but found that the dense quilting added even more color and texture. I've never gone back to shadow quilting.

Computer printout for *Elements*.

Elements
Susan Carlson, 45" × 45", 1993.
Collection of Brenda Hambleton.

My career has been full of experimentation. I've never been satisfied doing something exactly the same way as someone else. Perhaps a decade from now I will still be happily creating fish and portraits. Perhaps I'll be exploring other techniques or even other artistic media. Who knows? I may even get around to that stack of clothes that need buttons and knee patches.

The Book

In this book, I try to simulate the process I teach in one-day workshops. Besides the technique itself, I teach my students to look at fabric in new ways. As discussed in The Thrill of the (Fabric) Hunt (page 29), fabric can be broken down into parts: color, value, pattern, texture. Large designs are made up of smaller patterns that can be extracted for use in unusual places. A single flower might make a nice eye; a leaf could be used for a fin. Often, you'll find that out of a seemingly homely fabric, a gem or two can be mined. This sort of discovery lends excitement to the process.

The how-to section of this book, The Art of Fabric Collage (page 41), provides patterns and a step-by-step guide to creating a fabric fish, as well as guidelines for other subjects such as flowers or butterflies. However, as the photos throughout the book show, fabric collage can be used for any image you choose. Portraits, landscapes, still-lifes, even abstract quilts can be created in the same way.

Two Snails Passing in the Night
Carey Armstrong-Ellis, 22" x 15", 1998. Collection of artist. "For a long time now, I have had a strange fascination with slugs and snails. They are slimy and repulsive, but oddly humorous at the same time. I think it is those eye-stalks—there is something disconcerting about having the eyes waving up in the air while the rest of the face is, well, down where a face should be."

Calla Lilies
Judy Marble, 31" x 25 ½", 1996.
Collection of artist. "This was designed and made
for my daughter, Pam. Calla lilies are a symbol of love.
I hand-painted the fabric especially for the flowers."

Brook Trout
Sarah Drummond, 17 ¾" x 13", 1999.
Collection of Mark Drummond.

You will find examples of student work throughout the book. Carey Armstrong-Ellis's *Two Snails Passing in the Night*, Judy Marble's *Calla Lillies*, and Sarah Drummond's *Brook Trout* are only a few samples. I hope the images will inspire you to create your own original works once you have mastered the technique.

Up from the Depths: A Progression Piece (page 83) provides an overview of the process I followed in a larger piece. This photographic tour of my latest coral reef quilt describes how I work, from the first inspiration and simple sketches through piecing, quilting, and finishing. It will show you that the artistic process is not linear. Even an experienced artist makes mistakes, has setbacks, and changes her mind.

As you read on, I would ask you to remember three things:

There are no limits.

All art is good art.

Ignore the rules—even the ones that I tell you.

Lime-light Lion-Fish
Susan Carlson, 16" x 12", 1995.
Collection of Cilla Stiles.

Echinacea and Black-eyed Susans
Susan Carlson, 12" x 16", 1994.
Collection of Sylvia Dyer. When we lived in Portsmouth, NH, one of my favorite summer evening activities was to wander down to Prescott Park's beautiful gardens. Somehow, the colors of the flowers seemed most intense at twilight, though it was a mid-day walk when I remembered my camera. This piece, and *Cosmo folia* on page 68, are based on photos taken that day.

Author's Gallery

Farmer's Market

Susan Carlson, each piece 13½ × 33¾", 1996.
Collection of Portland Public Market, Portland, Maine. Based on the farmer's market held every Saturday—May through October— in Portsmouth, NH. It's a color-filled event that I visited frequently while we lived there. Over the course of two years, I took photos with a series such as this in mind. The colors, shapes, and patterns created by the baskets, crates, boxes, and buckets full of food and flowers were too tempting to resist.

Redband Rainbow
Susan Carlson, 20¾" × 8¾", 1995.
Collection of Meta Carlson.

Seeing Spots Parrotfish
Susan Carlson, 23½" by 12", 1995.
Collection of Sarah Drummond.

Ramsey Children

Susan Carlson, 48" x 60", 1997.
Collection of Mitch and Nancy Ramsey. This is one of
a number of commissioned portraits I have done over
the years. I used three separate photographs for
the final image: one for the basic pose and the girls'
expressions, one for the little boy's expression, and
one for the flowers behind them.

Surprise Me

Susan Carlson 45¾" x 34½", 1992.
Collection of Thomas Allen. Years ago I threw a surprise
party for my husband. It was even more surprising when
his two best friends traveled a few hours to be there.
I took a great photo of them clowning around, being
buddies. It became the inspiration for Tom's (center)
next year's birthday present. The quote above Tom's
head paraphrases a favorite poet of his, Alden Nolan,
and talks of friendship and surprises: "Who know me
better than they know themselves, who talk, but not too
much, who make me laugh and laugh with me , who say
things to surprise me, occasionally."

Coral Reef II
Susan Carlson, 33" × 46", 1995.
Collection of artist. This scene was put together soon
after the completion of *Coral Reef I*. I had done so
much research and had so many images left over that
this piece fell right into place.

Coral Reef I
Susan Carlson, 57" × 38½", 1995.
Collection of Mildred John. Once I started making fabric collages of single fish, I soon wanted to expand my horizons into full reef environments. This is the first in what I imagine will be a long line of underwater scenes.

Scarab
Susan Carlson, 4¼" × 6¼", 1996.
Collection of Blair LaBella Brown.
Found on Egyptian antiquities, scarab beetles are an ancient symbol representing eternal life.

Ellis Reef

Susan Carlson, 144" x 18" 1997.
Collection of Mr. and Mrs. Henry Ellis. A commissioned piece, made to fit a specific space between glass doors and windows on a two-story wall. Though pictured one on top of the other for space considerations, this reef is meant to be seen end to end, creating a 12 foot triptych. When hanging in place, it gives the impression of a large aquarium.

**Midsummer's Night
Stream Fish**
Susan Carlson, 16 x 11¾", 1996.
Collection of Paul Rollins.

The Amazing Flying Blennies
Susan Carlson, 50" x 36", 1998.
Collection of Carla Rice. A cross between
a school of fish and a circus act. I wanted
to do a big, bright, and fun piece. I see this
as a family of blennies jumping and leaping
in the spotlights of the center ring.

Crescent Moon Fish
Susan Carlson, 20 ¼" x 14 ½", 1998.
Collection of Carla Rollins.

Yellow Streaked Pince-nez
Susan Carlson, 15 ¾" x 11 ½", 1998.
Collection of Thomas Allen.

Golden Swallowtail
Susan Carlson, 20¼" × 11¼", 1996.
Collection of Blair LaBella Brown. After a few years of fish, I decided to
expand my repertoire to include bugs. Butterflies and beetles can rival even
fish in colors and patterns.

Freckled Puffer
Susan Carlson, 31 ½" × 19", 1998.
Collection of Nanci Ricciotti.

Ocean-Tide Grouper
Susan Carlson, 16 ¼" × 12", 1998.
Collection of Samuel Allen.

Seasoned Scorpionfish
Susan Carlson, 21 ¼" × 15 ¼", 1995.
Collection of Barbara and Donald Green.

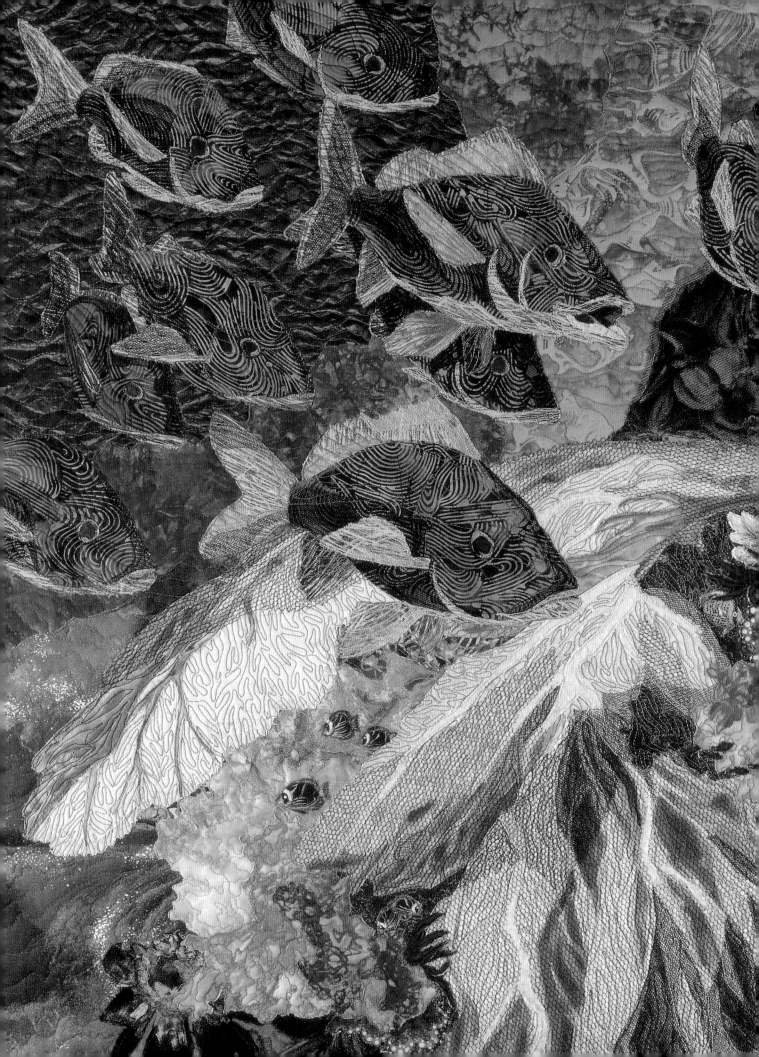

chapter two

The Thrill of the (Fabric) Hunt

I don't know about you, but fabric is why I'm a quilt artist. Fabric is always a joy to the senses. It delights the eye, of course, with its colors and patterns. But almost as important to me is the feel of fabric. I like working with my hands—I'm a tactile person. My husband tells the story of a visit to a fabric store, where as I fondled bolts of fabric, I exclaimed, "Ooh, look at this…" But I wasn't *looking* at the fabric at all—my hands were looking for me.

Our first response to fabric, however, is primarily visual. It is often an instinctual response—"Ooh, that looks good," or "I don't like the look of that." That instinct plays an important part in choosing fabric for any quilt, but choosing the right fabric for a log cabin quilt is different from choosing fabric for a fin or gills. You need a varied palette for fabric collage—a wide range of patterns, textures, and colors. The key to success in this technique is to train your eye to see the jewels hidden in fabric.

Pattern and Texture

The first step is to re-examine what you like and don't like. You may be limiting yourself unnecessarily. My first guild challenge required the use of a particularly "ugly" fabric. I was new to the quilting world, and was excited to see such a curiosity. I was sorely disappointed. As with everything in life, beauty is in the eye of the beholder. I did the challenge, and the remnants have been in my stash ever since. I can't say it's been my *favorite* piece of fabric, but it has found its way into a few pieces of artwork.

Coral Reef II
Detail, Susan Carlson.
A leaf, with a little forethought before cutting, made wonderful pursed lips on this grouper.

Coral Reef II
Detail, Susan Carlson.
See full quilt on page 20. Batik fabric with its naturally occuring color variations made a good choice for this school of grunts.

A couple of the swatches below some might consider ugly, but they have turned out to be extremely useful. They all played roles in my latest reef quilt, *Up From the Depths* (page 91). They also came to my fabric stash through varied sources. I never turn down fabric when it is offered to me—as with remnants from friends—and am always on the look-out for unusually patterned fabric found in discount bins or even clothing in thrift stores and yard sales.

Some designs in printed fabrics readily lend themselves to various elements of an image. For instance, prints of feathers or leaves make good fins. Collage a few together and you have a unique fish tail. Clusters of grapes or plump cacti can look like scales. Lines printed in the fabric, cut out just so, become the veins on a fin, or maybe eye-brow hairs in a portrait.

Following design elements on printed fabrics is a good way to let go and cut some pieces freehand. They can then be arranged and collaged in place to your liking. An easy place to start is on an

Evening Fan-Fin
Detail, Susan Carlson.
See full quilt on page 36.
A scalloped cloud-like fabric,
cut and glued together,
made billowy gills for this
fan-fin.

eye, especially a fish eye. The centers of flowers, dots, stars, or medallions can become eyes. First, cut out what you want for the pupil, glue it onto another color, cut around the pupil, leaving a circle of extra fabric, glue the two circles onto another fabric, and on and on. The eye can become as big as you'd like it to be. More layers add more interest.

A "vintage" fabric. It finally found its way onto the underwater rocks as feather-duster coral.

This fabric was marked down so drastically that I couldn't afford to not buy it. The green leaves were the perfect shade for some lettuce-leaf algae. The fronds from a couple of palm trees became small starfish.

The sight of the big, loose polyester stretch pants that were made from this fabric was *almost* shocking enough for me to pass this beauty by. It made a great starfish.

An unfinished dress from a yard sale was the right color for the quilt binding.

As I refer to it, the *texture* of a fabric is related to pattern, but deals with abstract rather than concrete designs. Fabrics with texture *remind* you of water, trees, a mountainside, grass, bubbles, or hair, but aren't literal representations. It's mainly the visual texture of a fabric I'm referring to, but it could also be a change in the fiber or weave.

Metallic fabrics give a more obvious textural change, and add a fun spark of color in the process. I first used metallic fabrics in *Elements* (page 11), pushing that bright and playful quality in the faces even further.

The detail photos that follow on page 32, with accompanying fabric swatches, are from *Elements*.

Dain
Detail, Susan Carlson.
See full quilt on page 9.
One of my favorite examples of texture is a hand-me-down plaid fabric used in my father-in-law's face.

Be sure to check the back side of the fabric: sometimes it's as interesting, or even more useful, than the front.

Front

Reverse

Front

Reverse

Fabric from a 79¢ rayon thrift-store dress that looks interesting on the front (left) ... but it was the reverse, (right) that

provided the muddy and murky rocks for the bottom of *Up From the Depths* (see page 91).

What would have made a beautiful garment made even better seagrass, starfish, and various other reef growths in

Coral Reef II (see page 20). The reverse side (right) made a great background of rocky out-croppings.

Air

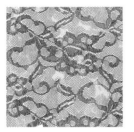

Pastel and gold lace.

A lacy sheer layered over other patterned fabric gives form and contour to Air's face.

Water

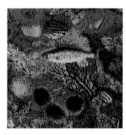

Shiny aqua spots.

One of my "cheater" fabrics provided a few fish for Water's hair, some more noticeable than others —little surprises for the viewer.

Fire

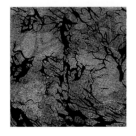

Shiny gold and copper.

This sheer chiffon adds color and movement to the dark area at the left of Fire's face.

Earth

Metallic leaves.

Another rayon that is as appealing on the reverse as on the front. The bright, clear yellows from the front side add life to the jumbled growth that is Earth's hair.

I find sheer fabrics such as tulle, chiffon, or organza very useful, and they come in a variety of colors and weights. I use these types of fabrics as accents to emphasize shading and highlights, or to add a touch of color over another fabric. Some of these fabrics come in different weights with different size openings. Larger sizes resemble scales on a fish. Tulle with glitter or flocked spots adds interesting visual texture to an area.

Creating Your Own Fabric

It may happen that there's a fabric you'd like to use, but you don't have enough of it. Or maybe you have a theme fabric, but the elements are spread out too far for it to work in your design. This collage process can now work to create "new" fabric.

For instance, I knew I wanted a starry nighttime sky behind the evening figure in *Twilight* (see full quilt on page 38-39), but couldn't find what I had in mind. The celestial theme fabric below was the closest I could find, but the planets were too large and distracting. To solve the problem, I cut wavy strips, avoiding the larger planets. I then re-assembled those pieces with glue to create a fabric in the scale I had imagined.

My sample fish in The Art of Fabric Collage (page 66) is another good example. The green background fabric had lizards that were spaced too far apart. I filled the "holes" by cutting out other lizards from more of the same fabric and gluing them down. After I quilted around them, no one could tell it had ever been any other way.

Thread

In the quilting process, thread choice can emphasize the fabric, or add sparkle and sheen. I'm attracted to the colors and sheen of rayon and metallic threads. But, until the fish came along, I didn't have much call to use them. Now I try to put a little glitz into every fish, be it through fabric choice, a glittery sheer, thread, or all of the above.

Twilight
Detail, Susan Carlson
See full quilt on pages 38-39.

Color

Don't be afraid to choose bright, strong colors. You see them in nature all the time. I'm continually amazed at the depth and intensity of color all around us.

A little research in books or magazines may prove helpful. Really look at the photos to see the color variations. Always take artistic liberty and emphasize the colors you like. Remember, brighter, warmer colors and more detail come forward—darker, cooler colors and less detail recede.

You don't have to follow any color "rules," but a knowledge of color basics can help if you are having trouble getting started.

A-luring Fan-Fin
Susan Carlson, 1999, 16¼" x 12".
My "how-to" demonstration fish in The Art of Fabric Collage is based on a secondary color scheme, with the additional complementary color of yellow to balance the strong purples.

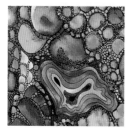

Here, a yellow "stone" makes a good iris, with built-in shading.

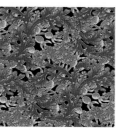

The purple and green of these fabrics work into the secondary color scheme, and provide accents to cluster around or between larger shapes.

Here, the magenta portion of an abstract rose becomes a fish's gill. Florals can be very versatile. Try not to think too literally.

Color is an immense subject. I'll just touch on the basics. To start, a color wheel can be used as a good reference to guide color choices. Certain color combinations tend to work well together. Basic combinations are primary, secondary, complementary, and analogous.

The *primary* colors—red, blue, and yellow —are often used together for a striking color mix. When two of these colors are combined they create the *secondary* colors of purple, green, and orange. We all know how well primary colors work together; secondary colors may be used together less frequently, but no less effectively. Either of these combinations has a lot of contrast and life to it.

Colors opposite one another on the wheel are called *complementary* colors. These combinations will have the highest contrast in relation to each other. Using complementary colors will result in a piece with a lot of energy. It is a good place to start if you need help putting fabrics together. Many of my pieces are made using complementary colors. A good example is *Twilight* on pages 38-39. The bright, hot yellows strike a balance with the cooling violets.

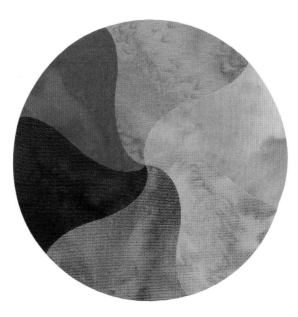

Color wheel.

Piscean Featherfin
Susan Carlson,
15 ½" × 9 ½", 1995.
Collection of Heidi
and Maia Carlson.
This quilt uses two pairs
of complementary color
schemes—orange and
blue as well as yellow and
purple.

Analogous colors are colors next to each other on the color wheel. These colors mix and blend well together. They can also give a definite warm or cool feeling to a piece. For instance, red combined with orange and yellow would feel warm, while that same red, combined with blue or purple, would feel cool.

Finally, there are *monochromatic*, or one-color schemes. It can be the most

soothing of color combinations—especially if you think of all blues or greens—or the most hot and lively in an all-red palette.

You can use these basic color combinations as a guide, or at least a checklist of directions to try, when you're not sure which fabric will go with another.

Evening Fan-Fin
Susan Carlson, 15¼" x 11", 1995.
Collection of Elizabeth Gilbert and Ned Loughlin.
The fish was created using an analogous color scheme.

Value

Value is the lightness or darkness of a color. In choosing a fabric, keep its value in mind, and how it relates to the neighboring pieces. When in doubt, squint your eyes. Squinting cuts down on the available light and blends different colors of the same value together. In order to make something (like a fish) stand out from its background, there needs to be a change in value. The less value change, the less contrast, even if you're using different colors.

Though overall it's a very colorful piece, *Elements* (page 11) also works with values. When grouped together, the faces complete the full spectrum of colors on the color wheel. But taken individually, each face is limited to a single family of colors—each is monochromatic.

Decide on the overall look you'd like. Are you attracted to muted colors, pastels, or brights? You may prefer stronger or gentler colors. Try to keep the intensity consistent to give your piece a sense of cohesion.

Messier
Susan Carlson, 27" x 36", 1994.
Collection of Victor and Wendy Kim Messier. Based on a photograph by Shuzo Uemoto. The easiest way to think of value is to think of black and white photographs, which deal only with value. *Messier* is a good example of using values to define figures. This commissioned portrait was done entirely in black, white, and grays.

Getting Organized

Most quilters are die-hard fabric collectors. They buy and collect fabric without even knowing what they might use it for. This is a practice I heartily support. The more choices you have, the better. For collage, you can never have too much fabric.

If you haven't organized your fabric yet, here's a good reason to do so. Arranging fabric in color families is one way to help you find that perfect piece. I also arrange my fabrics by value within the families—lights, mediums, and darks— with special piles for theme or abstract designs that don't have a dominant color. I wish the rest of my life were as organized as my fabric.

A sumptuous rayon, loosely woven so its color is influenced by the fabric underneath it. The intense orange blends with the bright yellows of the sun.

An upholstery fabric that served me well for angel wings (as shown here), as well as various fish parts, including fins and gills.

Twilight

Susan Carlson, 70½" × 50", 1994. Collection of Virginia and Robert Guaraldi. After the success of *Elements* (page 11), I wanted to continue that colorful and fanciful personification of non-human entities. I delved into mythology for inspiration and was led first to planets, then to the sun and moon. Two friends, Susan and her husband, Gordon, struck the difficult poses I needed to photograph. I then manipulated those images in the computer to give me a printout to work from (as I had done a year earlier with *Elements*). I see *Twilight* as a gradual and continual transition, a giving over of day to night, a balance between two beings.

chapter three

The Art of Fabric Collage

By the time I discovered fish, fabric collage had become second nature to me. I had received enthusiastic responses to my portraits and more challenging pieces such as *Elements*. However, it bothered me that many people I knew couldn't afford to commission a portrait or buy a large work. I decided that I needed to create smaller, more versatile pieces. I also knew that if I were to commit a lot of time to any new theme, I'd want it to be fun. Fun, for me, means working with vibrant colors and strong patterns. After some thought, I narrowed my choices to flowers or fish. I tried both, and, though I was happy with the resulting florals, the fish are my favorites. (If fish aren't your thing, you could follow the same technique as described in the following pages and try a floral arrangement or a butterfly as shown on pages 69-71.)

After six years, I've made literally hundreds of fish and—to my surprise and satisfaction—I haven't tired of them yet. I think it's my deep love of fabric—my "obsession"—that holds my interest. Fish, with their bright colors and astonishing patterns, are the perfect match for the wide range of fabrics available.

I started with what I affectionately call "flat fish"—a quilter's version of the classic trophy fish. They are bright, fun, two-dimensional adaptations of tropical fish. I concentrated on tropical fish

because, apart from their spawning colors, freshwater and coldwater fish tend to be much duller. After creating these fish, I moved naturally to coral reef scenes (*Up from the Depths: A Progression Piece*, page 83). These environmental studies are visually more dense than the single flat fish and I commit much more time and research to them. Creating three-dimensional scenes with realistic sea life has stretched me artistically. At present, I continue to work both ways, striving for a balance between the realistic and the abstract.

The Workshop

One unintended effect of my new subject matter has been to make my technique more accessible to my students. The human figure is a subject that intimidates many people—especially those without a formal art education. Fish, in my experience, make an almost universally popular and completely doable project. Throughout this chapter you will see examples of fish created by students in my "Somethin' Fishy" workshop. Many of these fish were created in a single, six-hour class. I am proud of my students and think their work, even better than my own, shows that the fabric collage technique is simple and easy to learn. As you continue, you will see how you can create a fun and fanciful fish of your own.

Getting Started

Through the years my students have possessed a wide-range of abilities—from seasoned quilters to non-quilters. However, they all seem to have one question: Where and how do I start?

My answer: Start with inspiration. Inspiration comes from different sources for different people. Personally, I'm inspired by the visual. I have drawn from books, magazines, even TV specials. Another source of inspiration is fabric stores. When I walk through a fabric store, I see fins, scales, seaweed, rocks, and ledges. Where one person may want to create a realistic fish based on a favorite photo, another may start snipping at her beloved fabric stash to bring to life a creature that resides only in her imagination. Either way can yield great results.

Supply List

• **Fabric.** You will need more variety than quantity. Have lots of pieces of fabric in the color palette(s) you would like to work in, especially prints. I find them more usable and also more interesting than solids. As far as color goes, be bold. Don't limit yourself to cottons if you have interesting rayon or silk pieces. (*A note on all fabric: You do not necessarily need to pre-wash all of your fabric. It certainly won't hurt, however; the finished quilt is not meant to be worn and washed, but treated as artwork to hang on your wall.)

• **Base Fabric.** ½ yard of muslin or other plain fabric.

• **Top Netting for Shadow Quilting.** This is an optional technique. If you would like to try this, you will need ½ yard of a lightweight tulle in any color. Usually darker colors work better. A variety of colors, weights, and patterns (such as glittered or flocked) can also be used on the fish for shading and texture.

• **Safety Pins.** For basting.

• **Backing Fabric.** Enough to cover the back of your quilt. The muslin mentioned will be enough unless you plan to add borders.

• **Batting.** ½ yard thin cotton batting. Larger if you plan on adding borders.

• **Thread.** A variety of colors to match your fabrics plus a few darker and lighter for contrast. Include rayons and metallics if you'd like.

• **Sewing Machine.** Must have the ability to lower the feed dogs or a throat plate to cover them up (check your manual or dealer if unsure). You will need a darning foot or freehand embroidery foot and #80/12 (average weight) needles.

• **Other Important Things.** Pencil, tracing paper, scissors (for both paper and fabric), straight pins, glue (I like Aleene's Tacky Glue®, available at most craft supply stores), reducing glass (helpful but optional), rotary cutter with straight and decorative blades, cutting mat, and clear ruler.

The Patterns: Breaking Away

To help those who feel most comfortable working with a pattern, I've designed three different fish (pages 44 and 67). However, if you're a person who doesn't like to work with a pattern, then don't— I don't. This process was designed for freehand use—the patterns came later. If you're most comfortable somewhere in between, you may want to use my patterns as a guide that you can vary as the mood strikes you. On page 69 I show how to create your own pattern from a photograph, and on page 70 describe how to freehand cut fabric for a butterfly.

For me, it's the fabric that's fun to work with—not patterns. In fact, you'll notice in my sample fish that I do not stick strictly to the pattern. Throughout the "how-to" I will encourage you to break away from the pattern as well. There are many ways to do this, but the bottom line is: Let inspiration be your guide. Your finished fish should be as unique as you are.

Step 1. Select Fabric and Prepare Pattern

As a preliminary design step, cut a piece of muslin or other neutral fabric a few inches larger than you want your finished fish. Then choose fabric and lay it out in the general shape of your fish. This allows you to see how colors work together. You may catch some problems before ever picking up your scissors, or you may notice a unique quality in your fabric that will determine how you cut out your pattern.

Folded fabric laid out in general fish shape.

Use a neutral colored background on which to assemble your fish. It will give you truer versions of colors than if you work on a dark tabletop. Muslin works well, and also later serves as a base to stabilize lots of small fish parts or slippery fabrics.

Fan-fin Pattern

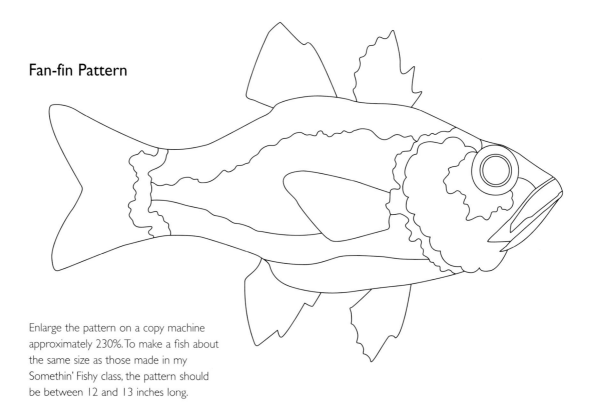

Enlarge the pattern on a copy machine approximately 230%. To make a fish about the same size as those made in my Somethin' Fishy class, the pattern should be between 12 and 13 inches long.

Do not cut the original pattern apart. Instead, trace individual shapes onto tracing paper, leaving cutting space between the shapes. Think ahead and extend lines where one shape may slip under another. Label each piece and mark with an arrow to indicate "up" before cutting it out.

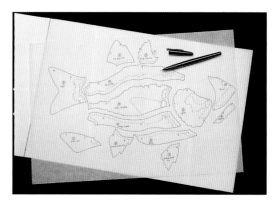

Redrawn and labeled tracing paper, showing "exploded" shapes.

This is an overlapping technique, not a jig-saw puzzle. When you trace the pattern, try to determine which shape will go under the other and add a little extra to the edge on the "underlapping" shape. The goal is to create a sort of "tab" as a place for glue to hold your fish together. This is the only "seam allowance" necessary. For example, fins and tails almost always work best when they go under the main body shape. So, on those templates, draw in a little extra (¼" is more than enough) to those edges that border the body of the fish.

Before you cut out the templates from the tracing paper, write a word or two on each to describe where it belongs, such as "belly" or "top, back fin." It willl eliminate confusion later, and, by writing a word, you will be less likely to reverse the template and end up cutting your fabric backward.

Let the fabric take precedence over the pattern. Let's say you have a piece of fabric with a wonderful shading of color from top to bottom. If you follow my pattern exactly, you may end up cutting it all apart and obscuring its beautiful features. So, instead of re-drawing four separate templates for the body shapes on my design, maybe you'd rather re-draw it as only one template for the entire body. This way you retain the shading or pattern that attracted you to that piece of fabric. Interpreting fabric in different ways makes your fish unique.

Solitude
Judy Warren, 14" x 15", 1998.
Collection of artist. By combining the upper and lower body shapes into one piece, Judy was able to utilize the rich color variation in a favorite fabric. She also added an extra shape of her own design to bridge the space under the fish's side fin.

Step 2. Cut Out and Assemble Fish

Place the template on the fabric. Use the transparency of the tracing paper to select the area of fabric that best suits your fish. Keep in mind color "spots" and contours of line in the print. Pin and cut out.

Template placed on fabric.

To give the impression of volume—for example, in the belly of a fish or the curve of a face—look for fabric that already has a value change in the design. You can often find it in batiks. These and other hand-dyed fabrics naturally have lighter and darker areas. By judicious placement of a pattern piece, you can create automatic shading, giving dimension and depth.

Susan Monjan's choice of batiks work very well in her fish. A leaf pattern lends itself to the veins of the fins, and another design became a beautiful gill area. This is a good example of someone who (almost) strictly followed the pattern. She altered it slightly to include a fifth piece of fabric that runs the length of the fish instead of the original four pieces.

Oh, You Handsome Devil, You!
Detail, Susan Monjan.
See full quilt on page 54.

When you cut out the templates from fabric, lay them onto the muslin as you would like to see your fish look. You'll be working back to front by placing the larger body pieces down first. You will layer subsequent pieces on top of the larger pieces. Some pieces, such as the fins, get tucked under the larger body parts as you progress. Placing the master drawing of the fish underneath the thin muslin will give you a guide for placement of the shapes. I decided that to best utilize the violet batik on the fish's underside, I should combine the two lower body shapes. Otherwise, the design I liked would be cut apart.

Fabric pieces layered onto the muslin base.

Billowy flowers become the fan-fin's gills. Cutting a promising section of the design from the fabric, it is arranged according to what looks good, and (obviously) not in strict accordance with the pattern. I had initially thought to eventually cut away the "brow," but it grew on me and, as you can see, became part of the design.

Gills added.

Small wedges of contrasting fabric define and accentuate the veins on the fin.

The top fin is placed.

Work from the back to the front of your fish. Cut out templates as you need them. This may encourage you to substitute a design in the fabric for one or more of the templates. In other words, you may not need to cut out every template. Maybe you'll find a striped fabric for the body of your Leaf-Peeper pattern and won't need to add the stripes I've drawn into the pattern. You might come across some leaves in a fabric that would make great fins, and use them instead of the given fin shapes.

Don't be afraid to cut out a piece of fabric and eventually discard it in favor of yet another selection. In this case, I tried alternate fabrics for the side fin, top front fin, and mouth. Eventually, I chose the bottom version. Remember, these are small pieces of fabric, and changing your mind does not represent a large loss of time or material. Besides, it's all part of the process of search and discovery.

After you have the main pattern pieces cut from fabric, you can start to analyze how it's progressing. Maybe there's a piece that stands out from all the others. Maybe you like it, and maybe you don't. If you don't, then the options are to replace it, add more of it somewhere else (if you reflect a color or texture in three places it often creates a nice balance), or blend it in by adding "transitional" shapes.

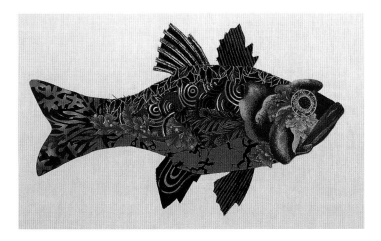

"Trying on" different fabric pieces.

Final fabric choices made.

When cut out and collaged in place, small prints in fabric—such as the seaweed pattern in this sample—can provide a transitional softening or bridge effect between two or more pieces of fabric. Some good ideas are leaves, squiggles, spirals, or flowers.

Transitional shapes added

Shading can be created by adding tulle or other sheer fabrics. In addition to various colors, flocked, sparkled, and starred netting is available that can add interesting spots on your fish. Note: This step is separate from the shadow quilting process described on page 55.

Netting in place.

If you ever get stuck, try looking at your fish from a different perspective, such as from across the room, in a mirror, by squinting your eyes, or upside down. A reducing glass is a handy tool for seeing your work in a different scale. It looks like a magnifying glass, but reduces rather than enlarges an image. They are available at many fabric stores and craft stores.

Step 3. Glue Fish Pieces Together

When you get to a point where you're happy with what's developing but you're afraid pieces will move out of place, you should begin gluing. I like a tacky glue such as Aleene's; I've found it is more flexible after it dries than other glues. Using a very small amount of glue, squeeze it onto your finger or scrap paper first, then dab it onto the fabric piece. You don't have to coat the entire underside, just hit a few key spots. Don't apply the glue too thickly, or it will bleed through and discolor your fabric. The idea is to just hold pieces in place until you have a chance to quilt them down.

Use one hand to stabilize a fabric piece while your other hand glues.

You may end up with quite a few layers by the time you're done. I've never had a problem with glue build-up or with quilting when the glue is applied in this light manner. The only time I've had difficulty with quilting is when I used multiple layers of upholstery fabrics, so you might want to keep those to a minimum.

When gluing down sheer fabrics, I try to find an inconspicuous place to dab a little glue. Often it's between two other pieces (for example, between the fin and body, as shown here), trapping the netting, so you don't risk seeing the glue. Other times, I look for a lightly colored area on the underlying fabric and add a touch of glue to press the sheer piece onto. The lighter color helps hide the spot of glue.

Gluing a layer of sheer fabric between pieces.

If you are concerned the glue will show, do a test patch with scrap fabric. As a last resort, the sheer can be basted, or even pre-stitched, in place prior to quilting.

Once your fish is glued together, it's time to select a background. If you assembled the fish onto muslin, cut it away from the back so you don't see any muslin from the front. Now you have a floppy fish that can be placed on a variety of possible backgrounds.

Cutting muslin away from the back of the fish.

The fish is assembled from bottom to top, but you should glue from top to bottom so as not to disturb the layers. There are two options for gluing. One is to glue all the pieces to the muslin backing. The other is to glue it all to itself. The latter method works well if you have one or two large shapes for the fish body. All the shapes should either fit under or over another, so it's just a matter of applying a bit of glue to those "tabs" to hold them in place. If you glue onto the muslin, avoid applying glue to the very outer edges of the fish. This will make it easier to cut away the muslin.

Step 4. Create a Background

I design a background the same way I start a fish: by laying down folded fabrics to give me a quick idea of how they're working together. I advise students to wait until their fish is complete before committing to a background. Very often your choices will change once the fish is finished. For example, the background pictured here was the one I had in mind when I first started. When I laid my fish on top, however, the background seemed too busy and the bottom fabric was too dark. So I pursued other options.

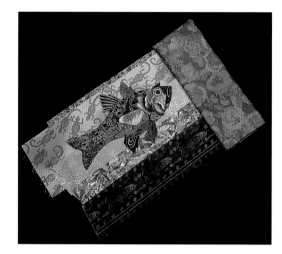

Original background idea.

Next, I tried a monochromatic color combination, keeping to purples in general. It looked all right.

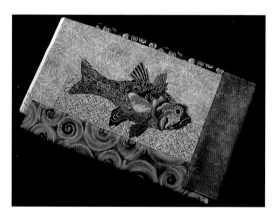

Monochromatic background.

One last try, which combined a little of each of the previous backgrounds with a little orange at the top. I liked it the best.

Once the selection is decided, iron and cut the fabric to the desired size. I've chosen four strips, but you might choose fewer (or more!). If there's any piecing to do, then *continue using the same gluing process as with the fish!* There's no need to go back to traditional piecing. Keep collaging.

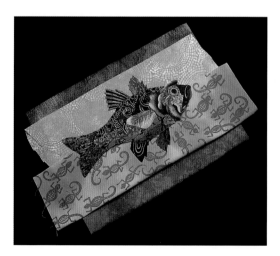

Final background.

Lisa Eaton thinks she is timid with color, so this fish challenged her to let go of those color inhibitions. Her favorite part is the gills. To construct them, she cut tiger stripes from a wild animal print fabric. To finish, she chose complementary colors—opposites on the color wheel. The fish is primarily yellow and orange with a hint of red. Her background choices of purple, blue, and a touch of green in the triangle border are perfect complementary matches.

Fan-Fin Fish
Lisa Eaton,
19¼" × 12½", 1999.
Collection of artist.

With a bold and graphic look, Jen Lyon's fish somewhat reverses the colors Lisa used, mixing purples and aquas into a sea of yellow-orange. She also collaged cloud fabric for the gills, keeping a couple of stars in place, which added a touch of whimsy.

Untitled
Jen Lyon,
18½" × 14½"
1995.
Collection of artist.

Another option for backgrounds is to work in contrasting values. Value simply means darkness or lightness. If you have a blue fish constructed from mostly lighter colored fabrics, a dark blue background would look good. This is a monochromatic—shades of one color—treatment.

The questions you need to answer are: Do you want your fish to contrast with its background or to be somewhat camouflaged? Do you want a graphic look or an environmental feel?

Backgrounds can be a single piece of fabric, or can be broken into halves or thirds, which works well for fish that have different values top and bottom. Another interesting option is to use scraps of related fabrics, pieced and collaged together as you did the fish itself.

I've found that hand-painted or batiked fabrics are nice choices for backgrounds. They have a loose and flowing feel that suggests your fish is swimming through a watery space.

Oh, You Handsome Devil, You!
Susan Monjan, 23" x 21", 1999.
Collection of artist.

You can jazz up your background, as Susan Monjan did, by the addition of various elements cut from other fabrics. Plants or seaweed, preprinted "cheater fish," rocks, even triangles, spirals, or "bubbles" can all add to the overall design and feel of your finished piece. These little touches can also reflect colors in other parts of the quilt.

Once in a while there's a part of the fish that seems to blend into the background (and you don't want it to) no matter what you try. In those cases, try tucking a contrasting piece of fabric behind the trouble area, and glue it to the back of the fish with a little of it sticking out. Then trim so a thin outline remains, separating the two areas for emphasis or clarity.

Step 5. Prepare for Machine Quilting

Once you have the fish glued in place on the background, the question is: To tulle or not to tulle? A lightweight netting, or tulle, on top of the entire piece will create a shadow-quilted effect. The tulle covers all raw edges and helps hold the various fabrics in place, requiring less quilting. Pictured is a maroon tulle on the left, black on the right for comparison.

Different tulles are tried on each half.

The use of tulle for shadow quilting simplifies the quilting process by smoothing over all the individual fabric pieces underneath. It helps create one consistent surface that the quilting foot will glide right over. It makes it easier to get used to freehand machine quilting, and I especially recommend it for beginning machine quilters.

Tulle anchors all the little pieces in place whether or not you follow the raw edges with quilting. This means that you can create your own quilting designs, such as scallops on the body of the fish, veins in the tail or fins, spirals, or waves, with little regard to the raw edges of the fabric underneath.

Please note: Tulle will slightly shade the image underneath, though the depth of the shading depends on the color of the tulle. Tulle comes in a variety of colors, and I recommend trying different options before deciding on any one. The best colors are often dark—black, navy, or maroon. Lighter colors sometimes work, but they tend to reflect light back to the viewer, dulling the colors.

Luann Udell took a wonderfully loose approach with her fish (page 56), using the pattern as a guide only and cutting the shapes freehand, including the borders. She let patterns in the fabric dictate some of her choices for the design. Using tulle over the top allowed her that same sense of freedom with her quilting.

If you choose not to use tulle at all, which is how I work these days, you'll need to double-check all the raw edges to make sure they are held in place with glue. It can be time-intensive, but the work pays off in the end when there are no loose edges to get caught on the presser foot as you quilt. If you like, frayed edges can be neatened up by trimming them with scissors after the quilting is completed.

Four-Fin Fish
Luann Udell, 23½" x 13", 1996.
Cotton fabrics and recycled
clothing. Photograph by Jeff
Baird. Collection of artist.

Safety-pin baste all the layers together
every 3 to 4 inches. You can easily remove
the pins as you approach them with the
quilting foot. I find thin cotton batting
works well for machine quilting. It's less
bulky and gives a nice weight to the
finished piece without too much texture.

All layers in place and safety-pin basted.

Freehand machine quilting tends to "shrink" the quilt as you move from the center to the borders. Since this distortion makes little difference on the fish, but a lot on the borders, you may want to plan how to finish your piece *before* quilting. You've already chosen your background, but are you planning to add borders? If so, do you want them to have a hand-cut, free-form sort of feel, or do you want them square and straight? If the "loose" look is for you, then add the borders before quilting. If not, then you should add them after quilting. In this case, be sure to leave enough backing and batting to incorporate any future borders.

Step 6. Select Thread for Quilting

When choosing threads, think about the final effect you want your fish to have. You can choose a monofilament or another thread that blends invisibly, or you can select a contrasting thread to stitch in final details.

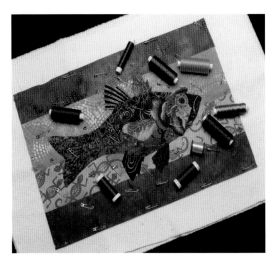

Thread choices laid in place.

I find these fanciful fish the perfect place to use those wonderful rayon and metallic threads, which come in iridescent and variegated colors. Go ahead and add some fun and sparkle to your fish.

When in doubt about color, use a thread that blends. You can always add contrast later, quilting over the area again, but taking out errant stitches is a time-consuming process that's best to avoid.

Since problems with tension are more common when you are using a variety of threads, I use a neutral-colored bobbin thread, such as medium gray, which will not stand out if it gets pulled slightly to the top. I also choose a lighter-weight thread (such as a "bobbin-fill" or polyester) so I can fit more onto the bobbin and change it less often.

Metallic threads can be problematic because they tend to break easily. Here are some tips you can try.

1. Loosen the top tension a half step at a time by moving the machine dial toward "0." Check the underside of your quilt for telltale loops that occur when the tension is too loose.
2. Change the needle—dull needles can cause a variety of problems.
3. Try a metallic or top-stitch needle. These needles have a larger eye and allow the thread to pass through with less fraying.
4. Try a fresh spool of thread. You could be dealing with an old or defective spool.
5. And finally, if all else fails, wind the thread onto a bobbin, and stitch from the reverse. To accomplish this, first outline the area to be quilted with a neutral thread. When viewed from the back, the stitches will define the space. With the metallic thread in the bobbin, and working from the back, you'll be able to add that sparkle to the front.

Step 7. Freehand Machine Quilt

As these student samples show, quilting adds both visual and textural interest. It adds details without obscuring the underlying pattern in the fabric, and it livens up an otherwise plain fabric. The beauty of freehand machine quilting is that your quilt can be moved in any direction—backwards, forwards, sideways, circles—in any design you can imagine. Since smaller quilts are easier to manipulate, these fish make a nice-sized project, especially for beginning machine quilters.

Solitude, detail, Judy Warren. See full quilt on page 45.

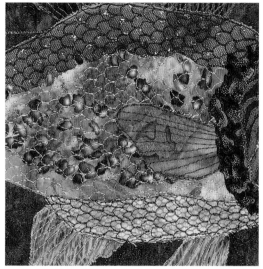

Fan-Fin Fish, detail, Lisa Eaton. See full quilt on page 53.

First, lower the feed dogs (or cover them with a throat plate as dictated by your machine). By lowering the feed dogs, you are in control of the fabric, not the machine. Second, you'll need a darning or quilting foot (see photo), which are usually circular or rectangular with an enclosed opening. This foot, when installed and lowered, allows you to move the fabric freely beneath it. Refer to your machine's operating manual to determine if your machine has these options. For some older machines, information about feed dogs and an appropriate foot may be listed under "darning."

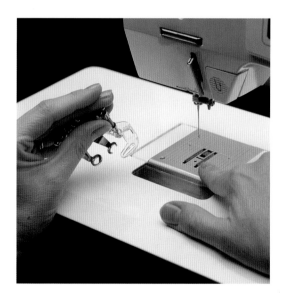

Feed dogs and various freehand embroidery feet.

The only other adjustment your sewing machine will need is to be set for regular straight stitching. The stitch length setting doesn't matter since, by lowering the feed dogs, you will determine the stitch length by how fast you move the fabric in relation to the speed at which you stitch.

If your machine has a motor speed adjustment, setting it to a lower speed may help your sense of control. At a lower speed, you can try "flooring" the foot pedal as you move the fabric through. Freehand machine quilting is basically a coordination of eyes, hands, and foot. By operating your foot on one speed you eliminate one of those variables and can concentrate on where your hands are moving the fabric instead. One student suggested that if there is no motor adjustment, a block of wood inserted under the pedal to stop it at a certain spot would accomplish a similar effect.

But whatever you do, don't forget to lower the presser foot before starting. It's easy to forget, since the fabric moves freely under the foot regardless if it's up or down. If you start sewing and there's a lack of tension, or the threads have tangled, check this simple solution first. Note: The presser foot should be up when *threading* the machine.

Practice on a test sandwich of the fabrics and batting you are using before moving on to your fish. As with any other skill, a little practice goes a long way. Feel free to experiment with a number of patterns. Pretend that you're doodling, except in this case it's with thread on fabric.

Test sandwich with sample doodles.

Your test runs should include moving the fabric in circles, zig-zags, and tracing a drawn shape or a design that's printed on the fabric. Moving side-to-side is a good exercise since it's an "unnatural" way to move on the machine.

Another test is to run the machine fast while you move the fabric slowly, and vice-versa. This way you'll see what your optimum speed is. Different people are comfortable at different speeds. Try to stitch as fast as is comfortable. It's hard to get all the stitches the same length, and I really don't think that it's all that important. Given a choice, I would choose smaller stitches over larger ones, and they're formed by running the machine faster rather than slower.

Most important, keep in mind that successful freehand machine quilting comes from practice, practice, practice. Just relax, have fun, and enjoy what you're doing. Expertise will come with time.

Where to Start

You should start quilting in the center of the quilt, and work out to the edges, just as you would for any traditionally quilted piece. You want the fabric to smooth out as you progress, and not get "trapped" between quilted areas. With my quilts, I don't necessarily start at the absolute center of the quilt, but at a centrally located area. With fish projects, I'll usually start somewhere mid-body.

Bobbin thread is brought to the top.

Bring the bobbin thread up to the top of the piece, as if you were threading a bobbin. Gently hold the two threads to the back as you take a few stitches in place to lock and secure the threads. As you start to move away, trim the threads at fabric level.

When you've reached the end of your quilting line, stitch in place a few times to secure the threads. Raise the needle and move away, first snipping off the top thread, then the bobbin thread.

This simple step of bringing the bobbin thread to the top of the quilt can eliminate a major source of frustration. Usually the feed dogs are moving the fabric away from the loose threads before they have a chance to tangle, but in this case, those threads may tangle as soon as you start because you're stitching in place.

When you want to stop the machine, try to do it with the needle still in the fabric so it holds your place. When you start up again there won't be a jump in the stitches. Some machines have a setting that automatically stops the needle in either the down or up position. For other machines, you need to manually move the fly wheel so the needle sinks into the fabric. Either way, it's a good habit to get into.

To travel from one spot to another using the same color thread, stitch in place as you would if you were ending that color, raise the needle and presser foot, and, *without cutting the threads*, move to where the other shape is. Lower the presser foot and needle into the new spot, stitch in place a

Needle and thread sunk in fabric after jumping over an area.

few times, and move on with the quilting. The threads can then all be cut at the same time when you move on to your next thread color.

If you can, it's easier to first try to find a "connecting path" between shapes. Sometimes you can hide the stitches along an edge or in a print, other times creating a quilted "flourish" from shape to shape. Either way, continuing to stitch between shapes eliminates the stops, starts, and resulting thread trims.

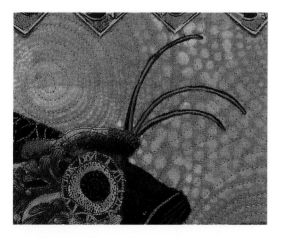

A-luring Fan-Fin
Detail, background, Susan Carlson. See full quilt on page 66.

Solitude
Detail, background, Judy Warren. See full quilt on page 45.

Large open areas often need a general allover quilting design. Free-form "stippling" is a common choice, and this is where your doodle practice really comes in handy.

I've found that pre-planning my quilting route helps to save me momentary disorientation as the machine is stitching away. It can be as simple as tracing my finger along the path I have in mind, or doodling the quilting pattern I want onto paper first. I think it helps to familiarize your eyes with what you want your hands to do, and makes it easier for you to visually transfer that design onto your quilt.

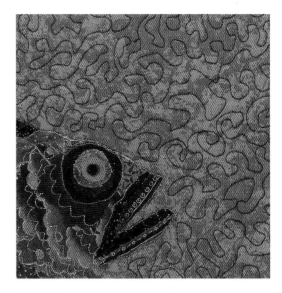

Untitled
Detail, background, Jen Lyon. See full quilt on page 53.

I always find it interesting to see the quilted design on the reverse. It illustrates my quilting choices better than any words could.

The quilting looks great from the back!

Step 8. Finishing Options

After you've finished quilting, lightly press with a *cool* iron and square up by using a wide or square transparent rule and a fine-line permanent marker. Draw a light line along the edges where you want to crop it. Once I know where those finished edges will be, I often add final embellishments with small fabric triangles or other shapes.

If you plan to add a border, use the pen lines as guidelines to align the quilt top with the border strips. Stitch borders, right sides together, onto the quilt. When turned and lightly pressed again, you will have straight, clean edges that disguise any unevenness that occurred with quilting.

Squaring up with a pen.

I usually choose not to use borders and use the drawn line as a cutting line instead. But in either case, trim to a final, clean edge with a rotary cutter.

Trimming with a rotary cutter.

Finishing for Framing Under Glass

Most of my smaller fish quilts are framed under glass. Since they won't be handled, I add a decorative wavy raw edge. First, cut strips of fabric about 1"-wide and glue them, as shown here, right side up under the edges of the quilt; about ½" of the edge strip should be visible from the top of the quilt.

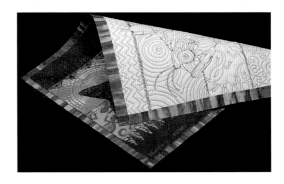

Glue fabric strips to the underside.

After the glue dries, finish the raw edge between the quilt and edge strip with a decorative machine stitch and press smooth. Then, using a clear ruler and a rotary cutter with a decorative-edged blade, trim it to the desired width.

From this point it goes to your picture framer. There are too many options to cover, but framing does add a nice finished quality to your work. To show off a decorative edge, float the fish on the mat board. Matting choice can reflect colors you've used in the piece, or create a more neutral "sea." Be sure to use spacers or the appropriate mats to keep the glass from pressing onto the quilt.

Decorative stitching is complete; quilt is ready to be trimmed with a wavy-edged cutter.

Age of Aqua-Wrasse
Susan Carlson, 14¼" x 10", 1995.
Collection of Blair LaBella Brown. This is the original Aqua-Wrasse that generated the pattern on page 67. The "boomerang" fabric in his face inspired the additional accents of red throughout the fish, picking it up in the background as well.

Finishing for Hanging from a Sleeve

For a more traditional way to finish edges and hang a quilt, use a turned binding with a sleeve on the back. My reef quilt, *Up From the Depths* (page 91), is finished in such a manner.

For *Up From the Depths*, I cut binding fabric into 4"-wide strips and pressed them in half, *wrong sides together*. The next step was to sew these to the top of the quilt, matching raw edges. I used a very narrow ⅛" seam since I wanted a very narrow binding, but yours could be wider. I did the sides first, turning and ironing to the back using the seam allowance as a guide for width. After pinning it in place, I hand stitched the folded edge of the binding onto the quilt back. The process was repeated on the top and bottom edges of the quilt, with the following exception: I was careful to leave at least ½" extra fabric at each corner, turning it under to finish the end of the binding before hand-stitching onto the back.

Binding, sleeve, and wood lath for hanging visible from the back of the quilt.

To make a sleeve, cut a strip of fabric 6" wide or more, and as long as the width of the quilt. Turn under and finish off the short edges so its finished length is a couple of inches shorter than the quilt width. Match the long edges, right sides together, and stitch closed. Turn and press flat. Center the sleeve on the back of the quilt, about ¼" or so from the top. Hand stitch in place, top and bottom. To hang, insert a dowel or wood lath that is slightly longer than the sleeve, but which doesn't extend beyond the binding.

Final Steps

Sign and date your quilt; you could also name your fish. Since you're now an experienced machine quilter, try signing your name using freehand machine quilting (before matting and framing!). You could include a patch on the back that describes more about it or yourself. If you have the piece framed, ask to be called after the matting is complete so you can go in and sign your name and title the fish before they finish the framing process.

You should sign, date, and name your quilt.

A-luring Fan-Fin
Susan Carlson, 20" x 16" framed, 1999. Collection of the artist.

Finished!

Throw yourself a little party to celebrate the completion of your artwork. Serve fish kabobs or salmon paté. When I finish a major piece I invite friends over to celebrate. For instance, when *Elements* was completed, we had a pot-luck where everyone brought a dish symbolizing an element—bread for earth, gazpacho for fire, watermelon for water, and blueberry pie for air.

Other Patterns

As promised, here are more pattern options. I call them Leaf Peeper and Aqua-Wrasse. These patterns can be used following the same steps as described with the Fan-Fin pattern. To make a fish the same size as used in my class, enlarge the pattern on a copy machine at approximately 180% (12-13 inches). Samples based on these patterns can be found in the student gallery beginning on page 72.

Leaf-Peeper Pattern

Aqua-Wrasse Pattern

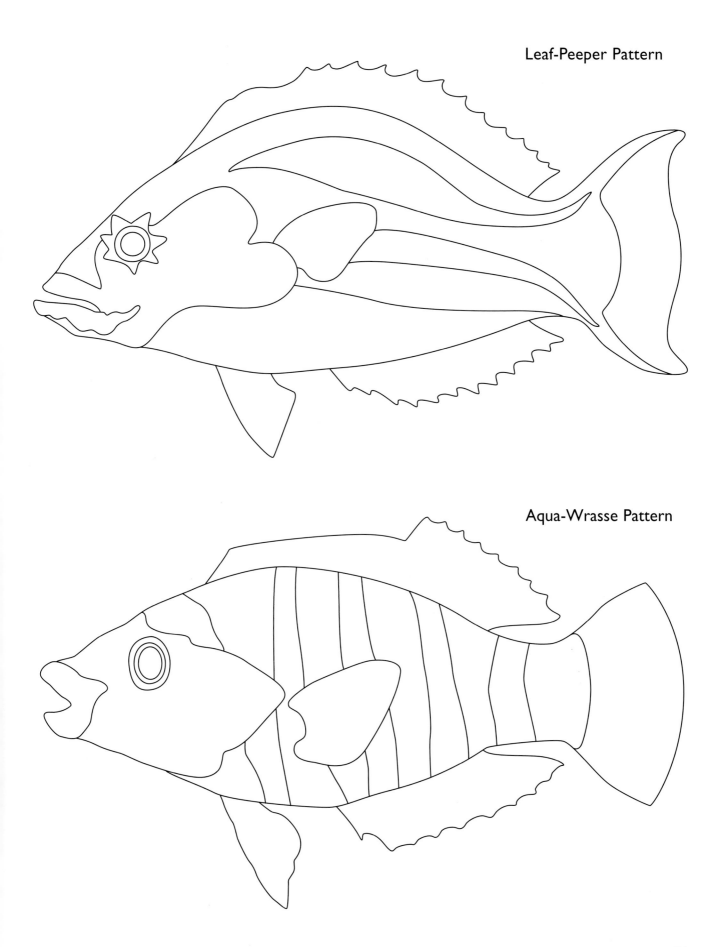

Cosmo Folia
Susan Carlson, 11 ½" x 15 ¼", 1994.
Collection of Heidi Carlson.

Make Your Own Pattern

Don't like fish? It's okay, really... If they aren't your "thing," don't worry. Perhaps you find flowers (or people, animals, or landscapes, and so on) more inspiring. As you see in this floral quilt and in examples throughout the book, this process lends itself to any subject matter.

To design your own pattern, one way is to start with your inspiration—a photo of a flower or a sketch you've drawn. Using a color copier (black and white is fine if you're working from a line drawing), enlarge your image to the size you'd like your finished quilt to be. Then lay tracing paper over the photocopy and make a simple drawing. Outline lights and darks. Simplify shapes by combining those that are close in color or value. Use another piece of tracing paper to "explode" the pattern into shapes you can cut out and collage together. Then follow the same steps I used to create a fish.

Original photo

Tracing of some of the lights and darks in the flowers.

Emerald Swallowtail
Susan Carlson, 13½" x 10", 1996.
Collection of William and Meta Carlson.

Freehand Cutting Your Fabric

Like fish, butterflies can be fun and freeing. They are colorful, their shapes are simple, and their markings can be mimicked by the patterns found in fabric. For the quilt above, I started with a base cut out of ochre yellow fabric in the shape of a butterfly. Next, I selected fabrics based on their pattern, texture, and color. I then freehand cut shapes and collaged them onto the base. By freehand cutting along the lines found in the fabric, instead of using a pattern, I created a one-of-a-kind specimen.

For this exercise, trace and enlarge (on a photocopier) a basic butterfly shape to use as a pattern for the base. Or, better yet, fold some fabric in half and freehand cut a wing shape on the fold (which is what I did). Unfold, and you have the full wingspan.

Once you have the base, find shapes and designs in fabrics that you can cut out to form the areas of color. A drawing or photo of a butterfly can be used as a guide for shapes and color spots on the wings. But let your fabric dictate your final choices. Don't disregard an interesting shape just because it doesn't match the real butterfly. Look for fabrics with symmetrical patterns in them—a shape you could cut out for one wing, then another that mirrors the image for the opposite side. They don't have to match exactly, just *seem* to at first glance. If you notice on my butterfly, there are slight variations from one side to the other, just like you find in nature. Nothing is truly symmetrical.

Again, you should train your eye to really look at your fabric and find shapes and patterns in it that are interesting. "Organic" and flowing shapes such as leaves, flowers (cutting one in half gives you two shapes that reflect each other), spirals, squiggles, and other "spots" of color combine well in such a project. Just let go and have fun!

Half of a Butterfly

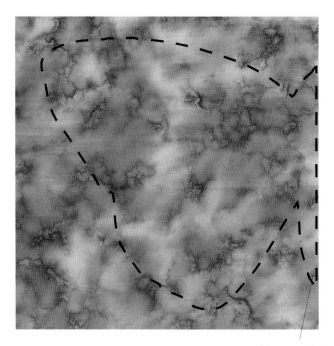

Place on fold

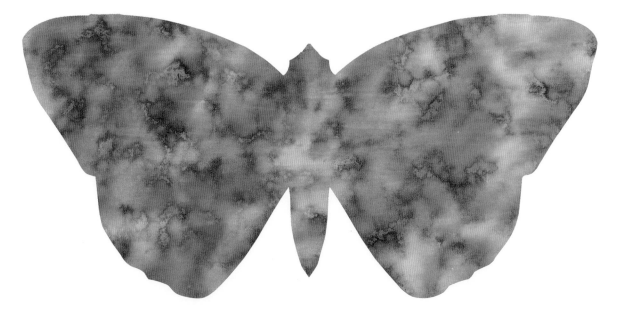

A whole butterfly cut from a single piece of fabric makes a good base from which you can build up layers.

chapter four
Student Gallery

Not everyone is a fish lover. I like them, and my students tend to like them too. However, as the following pieces demonstrate, anything goes with the subject matter that students have found to interpret. My students often use fabric collage as a jumping-off point for exploring other techniques, including beading and other embellishments. Some of these works were created in my classes—others were made much later. I am very proud to see this technique still being used years afterward. Many have used free-hand cutting for all or part of the design process. To me, each one is imaginative and inspiring. I hope they will motivate you as well.

Aqua Fish Fantasy
Catherine Worthington,
22 ¼" × 14 ½", 1996.
Collection of artist.

Lobster
Detail, Lisa Eaton, full quilt 17" × 22 ¾", 1995.
Collection of artist.
"I have always been attracted to lobsters. They're delicious, and beautiful to look at. As a resident of Maine, I see lobsters everywhere— on mugs, tee-shirts, key rings, restaurant signs, even on our license plates. When I learned how to use Susan's collage quilting method, a lobster was one of the first things I made."

Caribbean Fantasy
Susan Klibanoff,
23½" × 18", 1997.
Embellished with Japanese and Czechoslovakian glass beads and sequins. Collection of artist. "The Dutch Javanese background fabric I purchased in the Bahamas lends itself perfectly to the theme of my quilt and this quilting technique, which also inspired me to look at fabric in new ways as well. I've taken on projects I never would have approached with more traditional methods." Based on Aqua-Wrasse pattern.

Dotty John Dory
Carey Armstrong-Ellis, 17½" × 14", 1997.
Collection of artist. "This piece is based on a nineteenth-century engraving of a fish called a 'John Dory.' The real fish is probably brown and gray and certainly had no polka dots, but I decided to make it more interesting and give it dots (dotty) and crazy colors."

No Doubt, No Trout
Peg Laflam, 19" x 13", 1997.
Hand-painted and stamped fabrics. Collection of artist.
Based on Leaf-Peeper pattern.

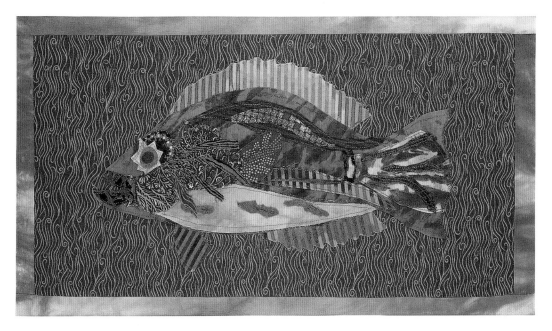

Blue Parrot Fish—St. John—for Tracy
Alison Banks, 19" x 11", 1998.
Collection of Tracy Banks. Based on Leaf-Peeper pattern.

Afternoon Buzz

Carey Armstrong-Ellis, 16" x 20", 1998.
Collection of artist. "When I was a kid, the seventeen-year cicadas emerged along the Ohio riverbank where my grandmother lived. We collected jars and jars of discarded "locust shells" and kept them for years, until my mother finally made us throw them away. I have fond memories of wearing the shells on my shirt and freaking people out, and of the thousands of cicadas singing in the hot summer afternoons ..."

Funky Fish
Elizabeth Gilbert,
17¾" × 13¼", 1995.
Collection of artist.
Based on Aqua-
Wrasse pattern.

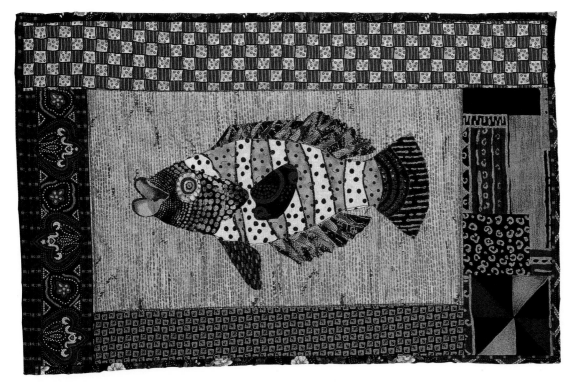

Aqua-Wrasse Fish
June Pease, 23" × 14", 1999.
Collection of artist. "My husband is an avid fly fisherman, so the Somethin' Fishy class was very appealing to me. I have pieced many a fish quilt and did my share of traditional appliqué fish, but this class opened up an entirely new technique for appliqué, allowing me to add even more color and dimension than has been possible in the past." Based on Aqua-Wrasse pattern.

Celebration of Stars ... Fish, That Is

Marilyn Follansbee, 37 ½" × 24 ½", 1997.
Collection of artist. "I took Susan's class in July 1996,
and in 1997 my quilt guild decided the theme for
their annual show would be 'Celebration of Stars.'
I decided to do something with star*fish*. The quilt has
approximately 64 fabrics with 122 pieces cut from
them. Each starfish was given a facial expression,
inked on. As in all my underwater scenes, there is a
cat trying to hide while watching what its next meal
will be."

A Fantasy Archerfish

Lorraine Landroche, 17 ½" × 23", 1997,
Collection of artist. Fabric collage, machine
appliqué, silk ribbon embroidery, beads, trim,
shadow work, machine quilting, fabric painting.
"The archerfish obtains its food by spraying
water onto its prey and thereby forcing it to
fall into the water where it can be eaten."

I Do That
Karen Fitts, 27" x 35", 1995.
Collection of artist. "This is a
portrait of my daughter's delight
and excitement with the water
on a lakeside vacation. A large
portion of the lake and border
fabrics were hand-dyed and
overlaid with netting for shadows."

Can You Fix It?
Amy Ropple, 29" x 25", 1998.
Quilted fabric collage with glass bead
embellishment. Photograph by Steve
Gyurina. Collection of artist. "This is a
portrait of my husband, Adnan Bozova.
The image has two interpretations:
Has he just broken the piece of pottery,
or is he repairing it?"

Schoolhouse Fish

Blair LaBella Brown, 12" × 15", 1998. Collection of Lewis and Mary Brown. "The Schoolhouse Fish has been around for close to fifty years in the form of a line drawing created by my father-in-law, Lewis Brown. Story has it that, when Lew was courting his wife-to-be, Mary Lanman, he paid a visit to her fourth grade classroom and drew the fish on the blackboard before her students arrived. The children were delighted with it and the fish has been making an appearance on any variety of family things ever since. For Lew and Mary's 45th wedding anniversary, I took the liberty of elaborating a bit on the fish and presented it to them as a gift. The possibilities are endless!"

Dos Picados

Holly Ranone, 34" × 29", 1997. Collection of artist. "After taking Susan's workshop, I was so inspired because I had finally found a technique that would allow me to create the pieces that I had running around in my head. But I had no idea how to put them together. Finally I was able to 'paint' with fabric with wonderful results. Each time I create a new piece of work I am truly surprised by the results, each new piece better than the last, with no limits to what type of design can be created."

Boo Boo

Amy Ropple, 41" x 43", 1999.
Quilted fabric collage with glass and stone bead embellishment. Photograph by Steve Gyurina. Collection of artist. As Amy says, "Domestic pets often live a luxurious but confined, harem-like existence. Boo Boo, a large and opinionated feline member of my family, is shown here reclining comfortably within a rich setting of velvets, silks, and stones."

chapter five

Up From the Depths:
A Progression Piece

My interest in coral reefs grew out of my research into fish. Looking for subjects to make into fish quilts led me into their watery world. Little did I realize how deep that water was.

Making a reef obviously takes more time and energy than a single fish. It's more than I teach my students to do. However, some do create their own versions. The basic technique is the same whether one is creating an individual fish or entire scene.

This chapter provides an overview of the technique and, hopefully, inspires you with the possibilities. It explains what I did to make this particular reef and the choices I made along the way. It does not concentrate on how I did it. For a detailed description of the process see The Art of Fabric Collage (page 41).

I'm constantly amazed by the variety of creatures coral reefs support. Despite the evidence in books and on television, it's

hard to believe that we live on the same planet as these strange and wonderful creatures. Corals and sponges come in every color and form you can imagine— and some you cannot. Fish such as clown fish, groupers, angelfish, and parrotfish display a wide range of markings— stripes, polka dots, blotches—all in colors that remind one of tropical birds. It is no wonder reefs are called underwater jungles.

I have never visited a coral reef in person, though I hope to do so in the future. In the meantime, I appreciate them from afar and honor them the best way I know how. I create these fabric environments using my imagination, to travel underwater with more ease than would be possible in real life. In a way, I do them more benefit by keeping my distance, since steadily increasing tourism stresses the reefs almost as much as pollution and global warming.

Up From the Depths
Detail, Susan Carlson. Full quilt on page 91.

Using Photos as a Design Guide

All the coral reefs I've made are meant to be as lifelike as possible. In this case, I've used the photography of a New Hampshire diver, Lee Cooper, for inspiration and guidance.

First I examined the photographs and arranged them in ways I thought might work in a design. I looked for colors and textures, close-ups and distance shots. I also kept in mind which animals would be found nestled among the rocks and which would be swimming in open water. Coral outcroppings were important references for rock formations and vegetation.

I wanted this to be a tall and narrow piece, emphasizing the light on the surface of the water, down to the muddy, murky depths. The photographs were arranged accordingly, with the clear light blues above blending into the rusty reds and browns below. These images became my guide for fabric selection.

The Sketch

Once I had a number of photographs selected, I drew some sketches, placing major elements in strategic places within the composition. The images that especially caught my eye—and that I accordingly made focal points—were the seaturtle, pitcher sponge, moray eel, crab, parrotfish, and barracuda. Other fish and coral groupings filled in the spaces.

I considered flow. Where was the emphasis? What would catch the eye first and where would it lead the viewer? Because of its size, I thought the turtle would be the primary focus; then, because of its orientation, it would lead to the distant coral outcropping. From there the viewer's eye would wander to the barracuda, twisting back to the face of the triggerfish and pitcher sponge. Finally, the moray eel would be noticed. Following its head down, the viewer would be led toward the rocks to end up once again at the turtle. I imagined a figure eight.

I also wanted to make sure the balance was right. The darks of the rocks at the bottom would be visually heavier than the lighter colors above. The seaturtle worked to bring some of those browns into the blue realm. Likewise, the frontal view of the parrotfish brought some cool aquas into a warmer area of yellows and oranges. I experimented with colors without disturbing my initial drawing by first making a few photocopies of my pencil sketch.

Playing with Fabric

Now I could start pulling fabric. Using the photos as color guides, and my drawing for placement, I laid folded fabrics into a general shape of the piece. This was another way for me to see how the colors were working together, and gave me an idea if I was missing any fabrics. Luckily, I discovered I needed a variety of aqua blues—a perfect excuse for a fabric hunt at my local fabric store! This was merely an initial selection that changed and grew as the quilt progressed. As you'll see, I managed to keep a count of fabrics used at each step.

Creating the Base

Number of fabrics used to date: 26

Since this was planned as a larger piece with many elements in it, I first cut a big piece of white fabric to use as a base. It also provided a canvas onto which I sketched the basic design; this gave me some idea for the placement and size of the initial fabrics. As these areas were blocked in, I pinned the fabrics in place, only gluing them down when I became reasonably sure of their size and shape.

Details of barracuda and eel with crab

You can see the sketching I did on the muslin in the background. The drawing helps more with the placement of the background fabrics than with the development of the images themselves. Within one or two steps the drawing is covered over. But it did help me realize that the crab was going to work better in the lower right than on the rocks above the eel, where I had placed it in my original sketch.

Filling In

Number of fabrics used to date: 48

For the most part, this blocking-in stage is used to establish the background that the creatures will be living in. But some shapes, such as the turtle and sponge, because of their size, filled the space quite nicely all by themselves.

I could already see that I was straying from my original sketch. The distant outcropping of coral became even more distant, but, that was okay, since the initial sketch was used only as a guide, not a pattern.

Detail of parrotfish.

I tried to keep all areas at the same level of development, though I did get carried away with the blue parrotfish. He proceeded to a nearly completed stage from the start.

Further Definition

Number of fabrics used to date: 70

From here on, I further defined what I had already started, adding some of the "mid-sized" creatures. Most of the additions were mobile—meaning they were constructed separately and could be shifted to determine their best location.

Little things like the starfish were altered and moved from the right to the left. Otherwise it appeared to be lunch for the eel.

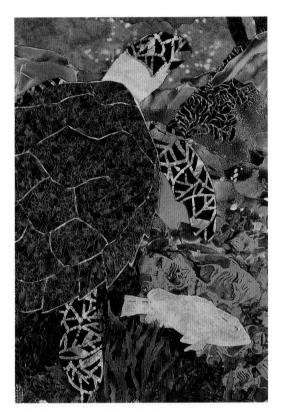

Detail of turtle and yellow fish.

I chose a variegated brown fabric for the first layer of plates on the turtle's shell. Further details would come later with a feathered fabric, which added highlights and mid-tones. The yellow fish was cut out and allowed to "swim around" until he found the right spot.

The Critique

Number of fabrics used to date: 96

I decided the triggerfish entering from the right wasn't needed. The batik fish fabric behind him added enough movement and interest to the area. The detail-rich lower left of the composition was balanced visually by the open and calm upper right.

At this point, I felt the quilt was ready to be viewed for feedback. I belong to a small group of fiber artists, and I took this to a monthly meeting. The suggestions I received were to add more shading and dimension to the turtle and the yellow fish, light spots to the rocks at the very bottom, and more detail to the centralized fan coral, plus tone down the yellow coral around the blue parrotfish. Those points, added to what my husband and I came up with, created a final checklist to tighten up the overall design.

Detail of barracuda.

The barracuda needed to look like he was approaching at an angle. The resulting foreshortening meant that his head would appear larger than it really was in relation to the rest of his body. I concentrated a lot of effort on getting the proportions right.

Finished!

Total number of fabrics used: 130

I finished the coral in the foreground by adding tulle for shading and volume, and bits of color for details. I also added "cheater" fish—small fish that I cut from preprinted fabric and wove through the coral, seagrasses, and rocks.

I resisted change to the yellow coral around the blue parrotfish. I had already toned it down once, but in order to accentuate the transition from light to dark, top to bottom, those particular yellows needed to be even more subdued. I substituted some of them with a leafy batik, darkened some with black sheer tulle, and layered bits of a paisley chiffon scarf over others.

I also moved the yellow fish away from the turtle. Since the fish is so bright, he changed the flow of the piece. The same figure eight is still at work, but the direction has reversed. After seeing the turtle, the eye is drawn to the yellow fish, then down to the eel and parrot fish, then up, and sees the barracuda last. It turned out for the best, since I liked the barracuda as more of a surprise.

After these and other minor changes, the piece was ready for freehand machine quilting. I sandwiched thin cotton batting between the top and a backing fabric. All layers were then secured with safety pins. I started quilting from the center under the turtle toward the outer edges. In general, I matched thread color to the fabrics. Only small areas, such as the fins on the yellow fish, needed extra definition from the thread color.

Up from the Depths
Susan Carlson, 29" x 75½", 1999.
Collection of the artist.

After quilting, I lightly ironed the quilt and squared it up. I bound it with a very narrow (¼") variegated blue binding. That particular blue spread the intense shades from the center of the piece into the lighter top and darker bottom, tying the areas together. The quilt hangs from a wood lath through a sleeve on the back (see page 65 in Chapter 3).

I like my reefs to reward the viewer with more and more details the longer they look. In all of the previous reefs, I added a small blue crab snuggled among the rocks. I carried the tradition to this piece as well. Can you find it?

Coral bed with parrotfish.

Detail of eel with red crab. and starfish.

Near the end, I added the red crab, in the lower right, as originally planned. It gave a touch of color to the area, reflecting some of the reds from above it. It also became something to catch the eel's attention. But unlike the starfish, the crab seems to have a fighting chance. After construction, though, he seemed too bright for the murky depths, so I layered a piece of black tulle over him.

I think *Up from the Depths* is my most successful attempt at recreating the feel of a coral reef. The vertical composition and the change from dark to light both work nicely to give an impression of depth and distance. Over the months of work on this piece, I grew very fond of the turtle, eel, and crab. Like any quilt I've worked on for a long time, I am almost sad that it's done, since I'll never do another exactly like it.

Coral outcropping.

Pitcher sponge with yellow grouper.

About the Author

Susan grew up in Wheaton, Maryland, just north of Washington, DC. She feels it was a great place to grow up since school field trips usually went to the national museums. She also feels lucky to have wonderfully supportive parents who were able to indulge her and her sister, Heidi's, creative desires.

Susan attended the Maryland Institute, College of Art, in Baltimore, Maryland, and earned a Bachelor of Fine Arts degree in Illustration in 1983. After a couple years of freelance graphic design work in DC, and various part-time jobs, she traveled to Maine on a summer vacation with a high-school friend. There she met a "really cute guy" who was working on his dad's fishing wharf for the summer. Susan and Tom Allen are now married.

In the fifteen years that have followed that first introduction (Thanks, Kathy!), Susan and Tom have stayed in New England. They lived seven years in Portsmouth, New Hampshire, making many friends in the rich artistic community. In 1994 they moved to Berwick, Maine, where three years later their son, Sam, was born.

Now they live just up the road from that wharf where they first met in South Harpswell. Two big ol' pups, Daisy and Hassan, complete their family.

Susan has received numerous awards for her quilts, including a New Hampshire State Council on the Arts and National Endowment for the Arts Artist Opportunity Grant in 1994. Her 7 ½ minutes of fame came in 1993 when New Hampshire Public Television did a short program on her and her artwork. She figures she still has the other 7 ½ minutes to burn.

You can view Susan's most recent quilts on her website at **www.susancarlson.com.**

Subject Index

Quilt Index

Self Portrait with Shadow
Susan Carlson, 22" x 36", 1991.
Collection of the artist. My cat, Shadow, was a
companion of mine for 18 years. While still in
his prime, I decided he'd make a good addition
to this self-portrait, playing on the theme of
light and shadow.

Other Fine Books From C&T Publishing:

Appliqué 12 Easy Ways! : Charming Quilts,
  Giftable Projects & Timeless Techniques,
  Elly Sienkiewicz
Art & Inspirations: Ruth B. McDowell,
  Ruth B. McDowell
The Art of Silk Ribbon Embroidery,
  Judith Baker Montano
The Art of Classic Quiltmaking,
  Harriet Hargrave and Sharyn Craig
At Home with Patrick Lose: Colorful Quilted
  Projects, Patrick Lose
Baltimore Beauties and Beyond (Volume I),
  Elly Sienkiewicz
Basic Seminole Patchwork,
  Cheryl Greider Bradkin
The Best of Baltimore Beauties,
  Elly Sienkiewicz
Beyond the Horizon: Small Landscape Appliqué,
  Valerie Hearder
Civil War Women: Their Quilts, Their Roles, and
  Activities for Re-Enactors,
  Barbara Brackman
Color From the Heart: Seven Great Ways to Make
  Quilts with Colors You Love, Gai Perry
Color Play: Easy Steps for Imaginative Color in
  Quilts, Joen Wolfrom
Crazy Quilt Handbook, Judith Montano
Crazy with Cotton, Diana Leone
Curves in Motion: Quilt Designs & Techniques,
  Judy B. Dales
Deidre Scherer: Work in Fabric & Thread,
  Deidre Scherer
Diane Phalen Quilts: 10 Projects To Celebrate the
  Seasons, Diane Phalen
Easy Pieces: Creative Color Play with Two Simple
  Blocks, Margaret Miller
Elegant Stitches: An Illustrated Stitch Guide &
  Source Book of Inspiration,
  Judith Baker Montano
Everything Flowers: Quilts from the Garden,
  Jean and Valori Wells
Exploring Machine Trapunto: New Dimensions,
  Hari Walner
Fabric Shopping with Alex Anderson, Seven
  Projects to Help You: Make Successful
  Choices, Build Your Confidence, Add to Your
  Fabric Stash, Alex Anderson
Faces & Places: Images in Appliqué,
  Charlotte Warr Andersen
Fancy Appliqué: 12 Lessons to Enhance Your
  Skills, Elly Sienkiewicz
Fantastic Fabric Folding: Innovative Quilting
  Projects, Rebecca Wat
Focus on Features: Life-like Portrayals in Appliqué,
  Charlotte Warr Andersen
Forever Yours: Wedding Quilts, Clothing & Keep-
  sakes, Amy Barickman
Freddy's House: Brilliant Color in Quilts,
  Freddy Moran
Free Stuff for Collectors on the Internet,
  Judy Heim and Gloria Hansen

Free Stuff for Crafty Kids on the Internet,
  Judy Heim and Gloria Hansen
Free Stuff for Doll Lovers on the Internet,
  Judy Heim and Gloria Hansen
Free Stuff for Gardeners on the Internet,
  Judy Heim and Gloria Hansen
Free Stuff for Home Décor, Judy Heim and
  Gloria Hansen
Free Stuff for Quilters on the Internet, 2nd Ed.,
  Judy Heim and Gloria Hansen
Free Stuff for Sewing Fanatics on the Internet,
  Judy Heim and Gloria Hansen
Free Stuff for Stitchers on the Internet,
  Judy Heim and Gloria Hansen
From Fiber to Fabric: The Essential Guide to
  Quiltmaking Textiles, Harriet Hargrave
Hand Quilting with Alex Anderson: Six Projects
  for Hand Quilters, Alex Anderson
Heirloom Machine Quilting, 3rd Ed.,
  Harriet Hargrave
Imagery on Fabric, 2nd Ed.,
  Jean Ray Laury
Impressionist Palette, Gai Perry
Impressionist Quilts, Gai Perry
Jacobean Rhapsodies: Composing with 28
  Appliqué Designs, Patricia B. Campbell and
  Mimi Ayars
Judith Baker Montano: Art & Inspirations,
  Judith Baker Montano
Kaleidoscopes & Quilts, Paula Nadelstern
Make Any Block Any Size, Joen Wolfrom
Mastering Machine Appliqué,
  Harriet Hargrave
Mastering Quilt Marking: Marking Tools &
  Techniques, Choosing Stencils, Matching
  Borders & Corners, Pepper Cory
Michael James: Art & Inspirations,
  Michael James
The New England Quilt Museum Quilts:
  Featuring the Story of the Mill Girls. With
  Instructions for 5 Heirloom Quilts,
  Jennifer Gilbert
The New Sampler Quilt, Diana Leone
On the Surface: Thread Embellishment & Fabric
  Manipulation, Wendy Hill
The Photo Transfer Handbook: Snap It, Print It,
  Stitch It!, Jean Ray Laury
Pieced Flowers, Ruth B. McDowell
Pieced Roman Shades: Turn Your Favorite Quilt
  Patterns into Window Hangings,
  Terrell Sundermann
Piecing: Expanding the Basics,
  Ruth B. McDowell
The Quilted Garden: Design and Make Nature-
  Inspired Quilts, Jane Sassaman
Quilting with the Muppets, The Jim Henson
  Company in Association with
  Children's Television Workshop
Quilt It for Kids; 11 Projects, Sports, Fantasy &
  Animal Themes, Quilts for Children of All
  Ages, Pam Bono
Quilts for Fabric Lovers, Alex Anderson

Quilts from Europe, Projects and Inspiration,
  Gül Laporte
Quilts from the Civil War: Nine Projects,
  Historical Notes, Diary Entries,
  Barbara Brackman
Quilts, Quilts, and More Quilts!
  Diana McClun and Laura Nownes
Rotary Cutting with Alex Anderson: Tips,
  Techniques, and Projects, Alex Anderson
Rx for Quilters: Stitcher-Friendly Advice for Every
  Body, Susan Delaney Mech, M.D.
Say It with Quilts, Diana McClun and
  Laura Nownes
Shadow Quilts: Easy-to-Design Multiple Image
  Quilts, Patricia Magaret and
  Donna Slusser
Simply Stars: Quilts that Sparkle, Alex
  Anderson
Skydyes: A Visual Guide to Fabric Painting,
  Mickey Lawler
Small Scale Quiltmaking: Precision, Proportion,
  and Detail, Sally Collins
Smashing Sets: Exciting Ways to Arrange Quilt
  Blocks, Margaret J. Miller
Special Delivery Quilts, Patrick Lose
Start Quilting with Alex Anderson: Six Projects
  for First-Time Quilters, Alex Anderson
Stitch 'N Flip Quilts: 14 Fantastic Projects,
  Valori Wells
A Thimbleberries Housewarming,
  Lynette Jensen
Through the Garden Gate: Quilters and Their
  Gardens, Jean and Valori Wells
Trapunto by Machine, Hari Walner
Travels with Peaky and Spike: Doreen Speckmann's
  Quilting Adventures,
  Doreen Speckmann
Wild Birds: Designs for Appliqué & Quilting,
  Carol Armstrong
Wildflowers: Designs for Appliqué & Quilting,
  Carol Armstrong
Women of Taste: A Collaboration Celebrating
  Quilt Artists and Chefs, Girls, Inc.

For more information write for a free
catalog:
C&T Publishing, Inc.
P.O. Box 1456
Lafayette, CA 94549
(800) 284-1114
http://www.ctpub.com
e-mail: ctinfo@ctpub.com

For quilting supplies:
Cotton Patch Mail Order
3405 Hall Lane, Dept. CTB
Lafayette, CA 94549
e-mail: quiltusa@yahoo.com
(800) 835-4418
(925) 283-7883